Make Money Online Entrepreneur Series:

Book 8
List Building
with
Facebook

KIP PIPER
http://www.kippiperbooks.com

YOUR FREE GIFT...

Want a free book?   Want access to more freebies and special offers through Amazon?

As a way of saying *thanks* for your purchase, I'm offering a free eBook that is only available to my customers.   Right now, you can get a copy of my book: *"28-Day Small Business Profit Plan: The Quick Start Guide for Business Success"*. This book is not sold anywhere else and can only be found on my website.

Plus, you will learn how to get instant notification whenever there is a new free book or special book bundles through Amazon.

Get the details at my website: **www.KipPiperBooks.com**

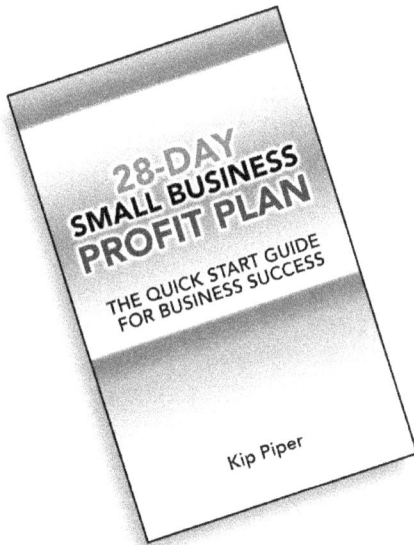

CONTENTS

AUTHOR'S NOTE

As you have probably experienced, the Internet and the websites on it are constantly changing. The information, examples, and screenshots presented in this book are accurate at the time of publication.

If you encounter any websites that have changed, please let me know by emailing me at: **kip@kippiperbooks.com**.

Remember, even though the website(s) may have changed, the principles, techniques and strategies in this book remain sound.

The links in this book are primarily affiliate links, which means if you purchase through the links, the price is the same to you and I receive a commission. This is the heart of affiliate marketing and entrepreneurship – which I am teaching you how to do with this book! I thank you in advance for using the affiliate links.

A FEW WORDS FROM KIP

Before I began teaching others how to blog and be successful with their online businesses, I wanted to be sure that I had something different to teach – strategies that are not easily found but can make a huge impact on success. The last thing I wanted to do is waste anyone's time. I wanted to offer something unique that would add both value and the potential for quick success for you.

Unknowingly, my research into online business success began in 1996 when I was first introduced to the concept of affiliate marketing. The potential for income excited me and I was quick to start experimenting with it. I joined Amazon.com and the few other affiliate programs available at the time. I added links on my website to products that related to my web design and Internet marketing business, with the purpose of offering quality resources to my website visitors and my clients. I encouraged and worked with my clients to include affiliate marketing in their overall online presence. I did this all in the hopes of adding to my income streams and eventually have affiliate marketing my dominant, if not sole, source of income.

But it did not come quickly, as others had promised or experienced. I totally, 100% believed in the concept of an online business and affiliate marketing (and still do), I understood the mechanics of setting up websites, creating products, and adding affiliate links, but I struggled with ranking my site high with the search engines and driving traffic to my site. Where were all the promised visitors who would buy what I offered or recommended so I could earn commissions?

Why were so many others achieving success? Why wasn't I experiencing the same success? Where was I going wrong?

I joined various mastermind groups. I purchased training programs from so-called "gurus". I bought books, read articles, watched videos, attended conference calls and webinars – I immersed myself in learning about blogging, affiliate marketing, and creating products.

The one most important thing I learned is that you need multiple websites, each focused on a different niche, to ensure a steady stream of income. "But," I asked, "if I can't get people to come to my first website, why should I spend more money and time creating websites that will not be visited either?" And each "guru" smiled nicely and said, "If you will upgrade your membership to our most expensive level, I'll tell you." But when I looked closely, I realized each "guru" was not living the life I wanted. In fact, most were working as hard or harder than I – with even less free time and income! They did not have the freedom of time and money that I wanted.

I didn't give up, though. I continued my search – knowing the one little "missing link" was out there.

One day I found it!

With this new knowledge, I knew without a doubt I could not only be personally successful with blogging, affiliate marketing and product creation, but now I could teach others those same strategies.

I realized that knowledge is what sets apart the training I offer – with this book and my other books which you can find at **http://www.kippiperbooks.com**.

This book is unique because it was written for *YOU*.

- YOU are someone who sees the potential in having an online business of affiliate marketing and product creation, but needs to know how to get started.
- YOU want practical strategies and advice that have already been tested and proven to work.
- YOU are ready for double-digit growth in sales.
- YOU are committed to following through with what you're about to learn.

This is why YOU are here.

Now please understand. Every piece of advice, strategy and practice has been tested on actual live blog, affiliate marketing and product websites – my own, my clients', and others. None of this is theory. You might then ask yourself, *ok, so how many blogs and affiliate websites has Kip done and what qualifies her as an "internet business expert"?* I think that's a great question. I wish more people questioned so called "experts" to see what qualifies them. As for me, I looked back on the last 15 years of stats and discovered that I have personally generated a 5-figure income in blogging, affiliate marketing and my own product sales – and that's just part-time!

If that's something you'd like to accomplish, you've selected the right book and series to begin with. I say "begin" because you'll soon discover that the learning process is a journey.

But don't worry! There's one more thing that qualifies me to lead you down this path – I'm just like you. It doesn't matter if you've never built a website or if you're already earning an income with blogging, affiliate marketing and your own product, and simply want to improve your sales. As you have already read, I've been wherever you are right now.

For anyone who reads this book and the entire *"Make Money Online Entrepreneur Series"*, and implements everything they learn, I can guarantee your business will move forward with more subscribers, sales and a stronger connection to your market. Like I said before, it doesn't matter if you've never built a website in your life or if you're already experienced, I've been there and can show you how to make blogging, affiliate marketing and product creation a successful income source.

But before we begin, I need you to do something. Connect with me on Facebook at:

http://www.facebook.com/TheRandomBlondeFanPage

I'd love to stay in touch and learn more about your journey.

You also are invited to check my website for more business books, and all of the books included in this *"Making Money Online Entrepreneur Series"*:

http://www.kippiperbooks.com

Thanks again for choosing to spend this time with me. Now let's get started!

"Done is better than Perfect!"

INTRODUCTION

This is Book 8 of the *"Make Money Online Entrepreneur Series"*: *"List Building with Facebook"*.

The entire series consists of more than 20 books, specifically written as an entire online business success training course.

Beginning in August 2013, I released one book a week, in the proper order to ensure success. If you follow the series from Book 1 to the end, one week per book, you will complete a 5+ month training course and master being an online entrepreneur! Of course, you can finish the series faster. Just make sure you fully complete the lessons in each book before moving on to the next. This way your success will be greater!

This series is carefully designed to give you every building block you need to build a successful online business. All of the guesswork is taken away, and by following this series, you will avoid most of the common mistakes made by new and even experienced online entrepreneurs. All is revealed – nothing is left out!

The beauty of this series is that you can pick up any book on whatever topic you need at this moment. Or you can purchase each book as it is released. Or ultimately, you can purchase the entire series in a bundle!

However you choose to use the information offered in this and the other books, you will be moving forward with intention and strategy for success in your business.

If at any time you have questions or desire personal one-on-one coaching for a particular topic, feel free to contact me at **kip@kippiperbooks.com**.

Here's to your online business success!

ONLINE BUSINESS SUCCESS CORE VALUES

Before we get started, it is important to understand, to be a successful online business entrepreneur, it is necessary that you stay focused on your business and have the core values that ensure that success. Here are the values that I have found to be essential to keeping focused and moving forward. These values will be at the beginning of every book of this *"Make Money Online Entrepreneur Series"*.

Be Passionate About Entrepreneurship

As it says, you need to be passionate about what you do and about being an entrepreneur. Being an entrepreneur will present the greatest challenges and the greatest joy you've ever experienced in the business world.

Commit 100% And GO FOR IT

One of the biggest things about being successful is being okay with putting yourself out there. Even if it's just a part-time business, commit 100% of yourself to the time you invest in your business. Commit to see it through and don't give up too soon. As the saying goes, "Don't give up before the miracle happens." Be patient and be persistent.

Build A Network of Support & influence

You must build a network of support and influence. This means building your Facebook community, building your Twitter community, and building your LinkedIn community. You must contribute to other people and help them be successful. By contributing to others and helping them be successful, you will become successful.

Get Comfortable with Being Uncomfortable

You're going to be doing a lot of things that you may or may not have done in the past. You can only grow when you're uncomfortable. When you're feeling comfortable and used to doing the things that you normally do, it's really difficult to grow, so you need to be comfortable with being uncomfortable see you can stretch and grow.

Consistent Growth & Improvement

It is important that you commit to consistent growth and improvement. We all need improvement especially if we are to grow and become successful, because staying up to date with the current tools and resources is essential. What helps you with consistent growth and continuing to improve is tracking your progress on irregular basis.

You also need to be okay with evaluating yourself and looking back at what you did and what you didn't do – without judgment. Simply observe and then recommit to the next step of growth and improvement.

80/20 Rule & Speed of Implementation

I'm sure you would've heard of the 80/20 rule (also known as Pareto's Rule) that 20% of what you do provides 80% of your success. So you need to understand that not everything you do is going to be perfect. Learn from it and move on. The quicker you get things done with the knowledge that you have, the more you'll be able to grow.

Flexible Persistence

Be persistent with everything that you do, and stay consistent with everything you do. The ones who experience the most success are the ones who are persistent in accomplishing their goals and are the most consistent in what they do. To be consistent, you must commit to regularly completing the tasks that ensure your success, whether those tasks occur daily, weekly, monthly, etc.

Surround Yourself With "A" Players

In business you deserve to surround yourself with the best and those who share your entrepreneurial spirit. You become like those you spend your time with. So choose carefully who you hang around with, so you are with those who think like you and make you stretch and reach higher.

The same goes for your employees. If you're going to outsource, you must select the best people who are competent and people you will enjoy working with. Avoid people who have negative attitudes. Surround yourself with those who embrace the concepts of small business success, entrepreneurship, and financial wealth.

Sell With Conviction

Be passionate about your product or service. Make sure you understand every aspect of it so that you can easily describe its features and benefits to your potential customers. If you have hesitations or doubts about your product, improve it so you don't have doubts.

Celebrate All Wins

Celebrate all victories! When you get that first sale, celebrate that first sale. Celebrate each new client. Celebrate each year of business success. Make sure you celebrate all wins. This is really important to maintain passion, momentum and to ensure success.

INTRODUCTION TO
LIST BUILDING WITH FACEBOOK

In this book, it's all about Facebook!

At the time of this writing, Facebook has over 1 billion users. The purpose of this introduction to Facebook – and as you can see, there are a lot of chapters about Facebook, such as, how to leverage groups, how to leverage your friends list, how to leverage business pages, etc. – is to help you get an understanding of how you should be focusing your time and effort on Facebook.

It's not sitting in your newsfeed and seeing what all of your friends up to! One of the things that is important as entrepreneurs and business owners is that we make sure we are monitoring our time and spending it very, very carefully.

If you are the person with in your business who is doing your social media promotions and social media growth, it's really important that you focus your time and time block all of the times you are on social media. It happens to all of us – including me – that we get distracted by social media. So it's important we don't allow that to happen with our Facebook promotional strategies.

Here is what's unique about Facebook. Facebook makes it really easy for us to connect with people when we acquire friends. It also makes it easy for us to build a Facebook fan or business page. One of the things to know about Facebook is that people on Facebook are not usually promoted to directly on Facebook.

What do I mean? It's not always a great idea to share a link to a sales page if you have a product or service that you're selling – or even an affiliate product you're selling – directly on Facebook. In all of your strategies in everything you do on Facebook, you want to acquire friends, you want to build your likes and the total number of people who are interacting with you on your business pages, and you want to also potentially build groups on Facebook.

But here is the biggest thing: Direct promotion on Facebook is not the best strategy. In everything that you do on Facebook as it pertains to your Internet marketing business, you want to convert those friends and those people who like your business page, and people that you are potentially with in groups, to your email list.

If you can have a nice giveaway or opt-in offer that you can share, that's much better than putting a link that is directly to a sales page, for example.

Your entire strategy should be built around those friends, likes, and the people within the groups with which you associate within your niche, to your email list. That's one of the great things about Facebook: it's very easy to foster relationships, but it's not a great place to promote.

So what do you want to do? You want to take those people from your business page, your personal page and those groups, convert them to your email list. When you give them the link to follow, you must make sure that there is an opt-in form on that linked page where they can opt in, get your free offer (white paper, free email course, free videos, etc.), and be subscribed to your email list.

In this book, we will talk about some specific strategies that you can do to get subscriptions, but for right now I want you to understand that the strategy is quite simple: You want to take your friends, likes, and your groups, and you want to convert as many of those people as possible to your email list.

This *is* the best strategy for leveraging your Facebook personal profile, business page, and groups.

OPTIMIZING YOUR PROFILE:
YOUR FRIENDS LIST

In this chapter were going to talk about to optimize your Facebook profile for your business.

It's very important to remember that there are rules against using your profile for monetary gain for your business. So you need to be very careful about how you talk to people on your profile about your business. But if you're anything like me, over the years you have messed in a lot of different types of "friends". So I have my family, my close friends from high school and college, people I hang out with now on my Facebook profile – but I also have a lot of people that found me and I friended them through my business.

*Facebook is regularly changing these rules, so it's imperative to that **you** stay up-to-date on what Facebook currently allows and does not allow. The information I'm providing in this book was accurate at the time of writing.*

As with most of us, my Friends list is comprised of a significant percentage of people that I really do not know very well. They've come to me through different things I've done on social media and I friended them. Some people decide not to have so many friends and they just keep it to only the friends that you know. That may be the easiest way to go! But since I've meshed everybody together, the key is to create "Friends Lists". When you create Friends Lists, if you can talk to different people different ways. It's a fantastic way to segment your communication on your profile so you're not spamming everybody with messages they really don't want to know. For instance, my cousin really doesn't want to know a networking event I may be hosting because she lives several states away.

You want to keep your communications really centralized in order to hit the right people.

Unfortunately, as we all know, Facebook is frequently changing their interface. So I'm not going to give you a tutorial on how to create Friends Lists. Instead, I recommend that you go to the help option in Facebook and search for "friends lists". When I did that while writing this book, I received the following options:

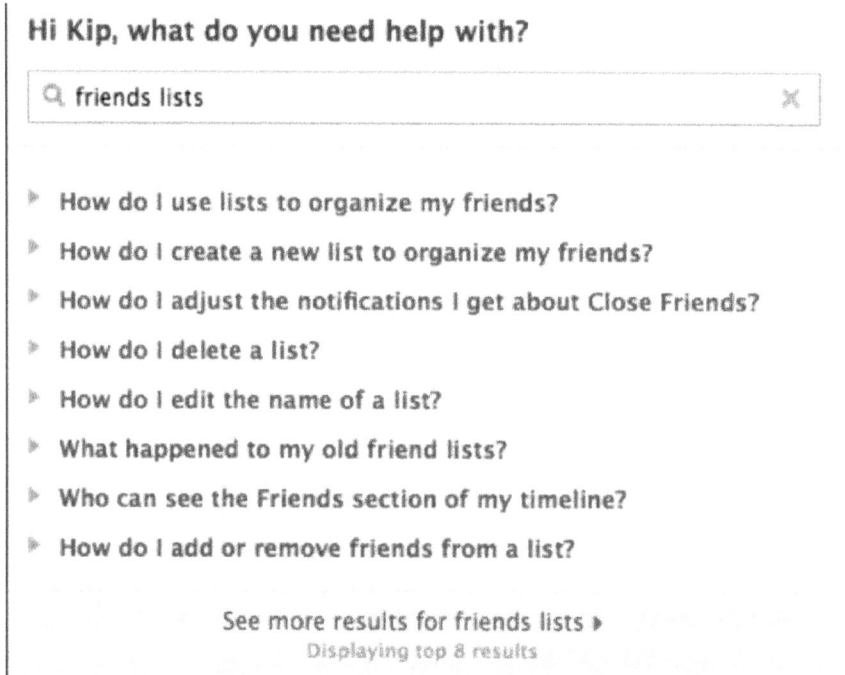

Hi Kip, what do you need help with?

🔍 friends lists   ✕

▸ How do I use lists to organize my friends?

▸ How do I create a new list to organize my friends?

▸ How do I adjust the notifications I get about Close Friends?

▸ How do I delete a list?

▸ How do I edit the name of a list?

▸ What happened to my old friend lists?

▸ Who can see the Friends section of my timeline?

▸ How do I add or remove friends from a list?

See more results for friends lists ▸
Displaying top 8 results

You can also search for tutorial videos on YouTube and for articles on the Internet. Be sure to watch or read ONLY those articles and videos that have been recently posted – preferably within the last 30 days – to make sure you were getting instruction on the most current version of Facebook.

In my experience, the best online course on optimizing Facebook for your business – and the techniques are regularly updated as necessary – is **Amy Porterfield's Facebook Influence (FB Influence)** http://kippiperbooks.com/FBInfluence. It is a small investment which will take you far beyond the basics that I am teaching in this book. This link will be repeated in the Resources section at the end of this book.

To get some free tutorials from Amy Porterfield, you can search for her videos on YouTube. However, these do ***not*** in any way replace her full course.

Back to the topic at hand.

As an example, let's say you created a list called "Marketing". Next you select the list. You want to post a status to them – so not everybody on

14

your Friends list get your status post – just these people in your Marketing list. These people are the only ones you will actually see your post.

So when your friends come to your Facebook profile page, they will only see this post if they are on the Marketing list. How do you do this? Let me show you.

You go to your profile or on your newsfeed and open the Status window, as you can see below.

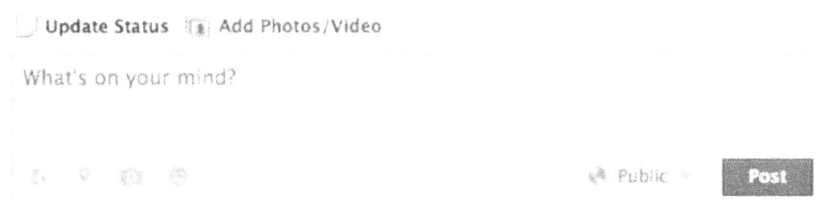

Next you type in what is on your mind that you want to share with your Marketing list.

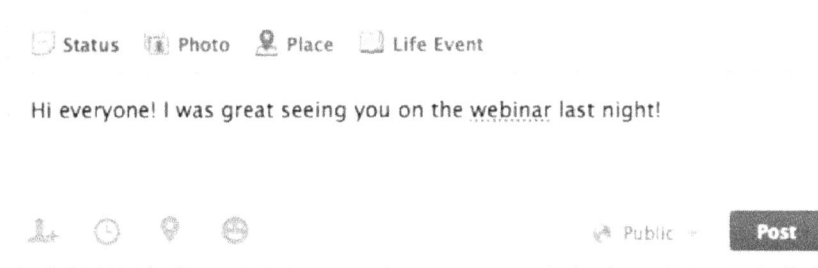

Obviously, you don't want to post that to everyone on your list because it wouldn't make sense. What you do is you click the Public down arrow in the lower right-hand corner, as you can see below. A drop-down menu appears and you scroll to the bottom and select "See all lists".

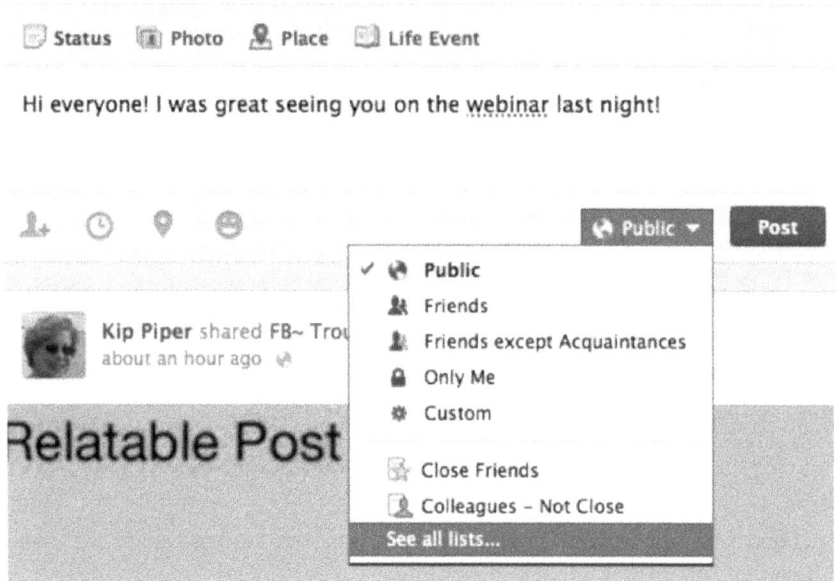

And from there you select a specific list of those you wish to see this post, as you can see I did the low by choosing the "Marketing" list.

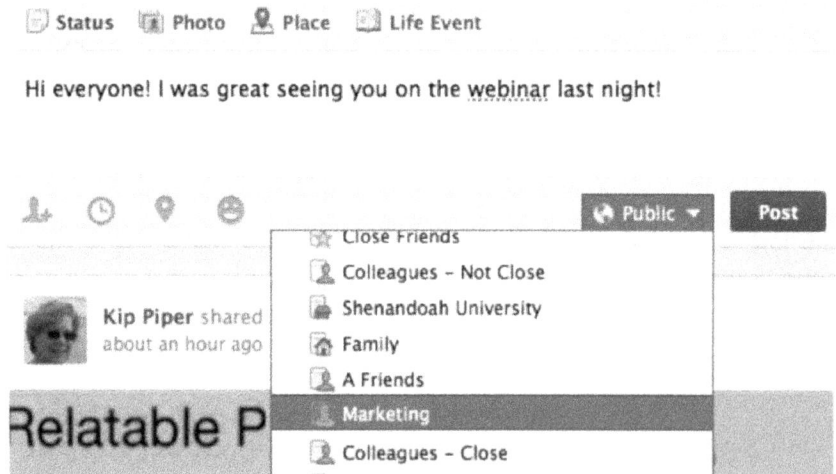

Once you have made your selection, you will see you the following message window. It is good to know that only the people on the Marketing list will see this post, and will not know how they are different from your overall Friends list.

What will these people see after you post?

When you share a post with a list or specific people, they will be able to see each other's names.

No one will be told that they are on your Close Friends, Acquaintances or Restricted lists. This hasn't affected old posts.

See what they see

Okay

So you close the window by clicking on "Okay", and then click on "Post" to post your message – And only the people on the list you selected will see the post.

Now let's take this a bit further. Think how great this could be for networking events you do, for people in certain areas of business that you do, etc. We are always so busy and we do so many things, so a great way to use your profile for business – and I say that lightly because I don't mean blatantly selling – for networking for your business, you should create Friends Lists. This is a fantastic strategy to segment your communication and connect with the right people with the right messages.

Remember, the interface appearance may change, but the Friends List function will remain available.

OPTIMIZING YOUR PROFILE:
YOUR BUSINESS FAN PAGE

In this chapter I'm going to show you how to create a Facebook page.

Many people are a bit confused about where to find the link to create a Facebook page. Here is a really fast and quick way for you to find the link:

Go to a Facebook fan page of someone or a company that you know **and** for which you're not the administrator of that page. You will see in the upper right-hand corner the button "Create Page", as indicated by the green arrow in Amy Porterfield's page below.

Click on the "Create Page" button and you can create a Facebook page for yourself.

From there, Facebook makes it very easy for you to choose what category you wish for your page, as you can see in the screenshot below. BUT FIRST, I say choose very wisely because the category you choose determines what areas of information you get to enter on your About link. That About link is very key to keywords.

For instance, if you have an online business and your About link asks for your physical address, that really doesn't make much sense.

So choose the best category so you can enter the most relevant information for your business.

As an example, if you're a restaurant, Facebook has an area where you can enter the type of food that is served and food examples. Obviously, you wouldn't have this area if you were a professional musician or a business consultant.

So categories matter especially for the keywords you can use.

Also when someone shares your page, Facebook will: different categories into that share contact. So you want Facebook to pull the most optimal categories for you and will do so if you choose the right category at the step.

Here is the screenshot that was promised above.

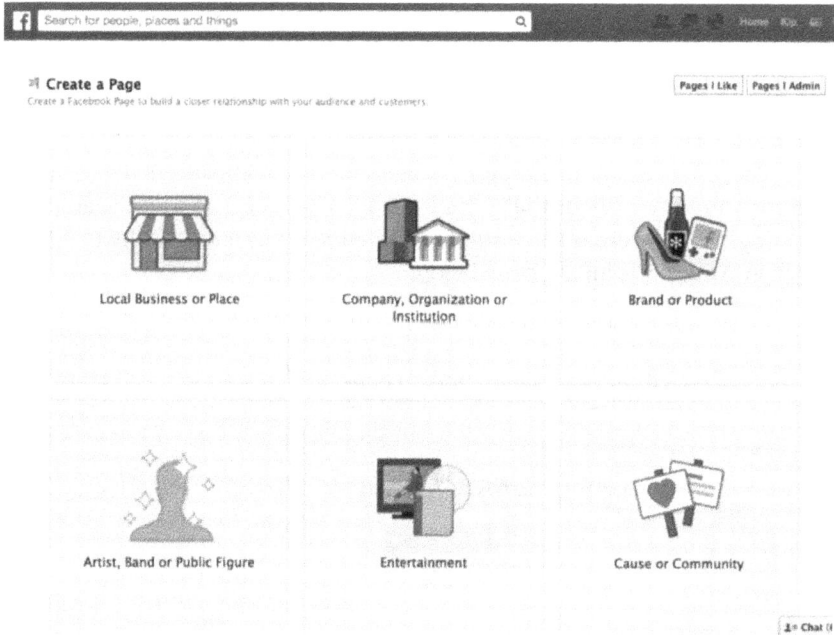

The different categories are:
- Local Business or Place
- Company, Organization, or Institution
- Brand or Product
- Artist, Band or Public Figure
- Entertainment
- Cause or Topic

The category "Public Figure" can be a little tricky in the sense that it is really more for celebrities and politicians. However, if you're a brand, or an entrepreneur and you are your brand, such as myself, it is best to choose "Brand or Product".

Let's say you choose "Brand or Product". Here is what you will see next:

By clicking on the drop down by choose category you can choose from a wide number of categories, as you can see below.

Once you have chosen your category, you choose "I agree to Facebook Pages Terms."

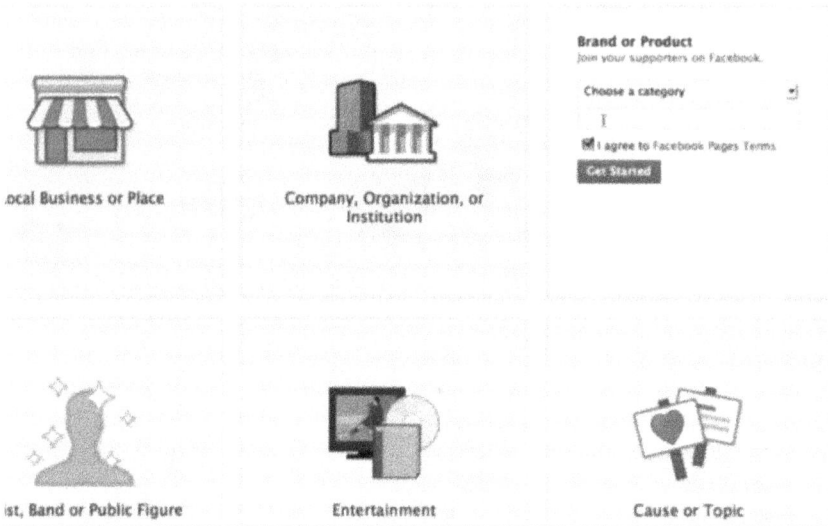

Then you type in name of your page. HERE, you want to choose very wisely. You *don't* want to make the name of your page keyword rich. That usually comes across to people as spam. You want to be authentic and use the name of your business.

There are other places that I'm going to show you where you can effectively use keywords in your page. However, naming your page is *not* the place.

You also don't want to name it something generic, like "Business Consultant", or "Gourmet Food", or "Internet Marketing". Facebook will shut down pages like that because they do not clearly represent the respective business. So be very careful at this point when entering the name of your business.

So for this chapter, I've created a page for myself under my name "Kip Piper Books" and the category "Product/Service". Once I click "Get started", the next screen appears, as below. So now you have your page. It's as easy as that!

Set Up Kip Piper Books

1 About   2 Profile Picture   3 Add to Favorites

Tip: Add a description and website to improve the ranking of your Page in search.
Fields marked by asterisks (*) are required.

*Add a description with basic info for Kip Piper Books.

Website (ex: your website, Twitter or Yelp links)   Add Another Site

Choose a unique Facebook web address to make it easier for people to find your Page. Once this is set, it can't be changed.
http://www.facebook.com/ Enter an address for your Page ...

Is Kip Piper Books a real business, product or brand?   ◯ Yes ◯ No
This will help people find this business, product or brand more easily on Facebook

Get Help Creating a Page   **Save Info**

So next I need to start filling out the different fields about my new Facebook fan page. I keep it simple at this point because I can always edit it later. As you can see below, I simply added some generic text in the description, I did and my correct website, and I chose my unique address for my page. For my page, I mashed my address to the name of the page. This is critical for consistent branding. And finally I answer their questions about whether this is a real business and if I am a real person.

Set Up Kip Piper Books

1 About   2 Profile Picture   3 Add to Favorites

Tip: Add a description and website to improve the ranking of your Page in search.
Fields marked by asterisks (*) are required.

Basic Info

http://www.kippiperbooks.com   Add Another Site

Choose a unique Facebook web address to make it easier for people to find your Page. Once this is set, it can't be changed.
http://www.facebook.com/ kippiperbooks

Is Kip Piper Books a real business, product or brand?   ⦿ Yes ○ No
This will help people find this business, product or brand more easily on Facebook.

Will Kip Piper Books be the authorized and official representation of this   ⦿ Yes ○ No
business, product or brand on Facebook?
This is a legally binding statement regarding the authenticity and representation of this Page.

Get Help Creating a Page   **Save Info**

Next I have the screen where I can upload a image for my page. I'm going to click the "Skip" button to skip this page, because I want to do the step later.

Set Up Kip Piper Books

1 About   **2 Profile Picture**   3 Add to Favorites

Upload From   Import From
Computer   Website

Save Photo **Skip**

Finally, Facebook asks if I want to add this new page to my Favorites on my newsfeed. I always add it to my Favorites because it makes it easy to access the page when I want to edit the page, post messages, etc.

Set Up Kip Piper Books

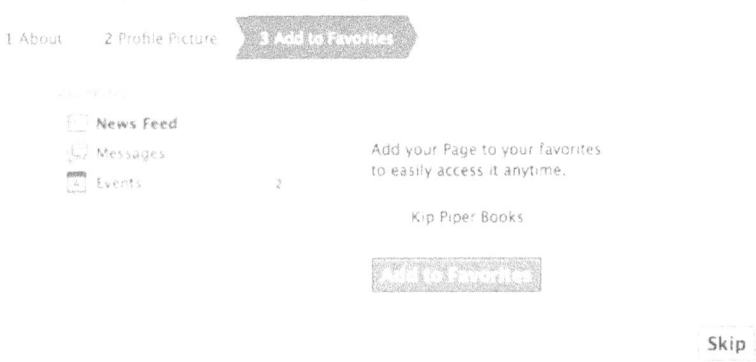

1 About   2 Profile Picture   **3 Add to Favorites**

News Feed

Messages

Events

Add your Page to your favorites to easily access it anytime.

Kip Piper Books

Add to Favorites

Skip

Now that I've completed these three steps, this is the screen that I see:

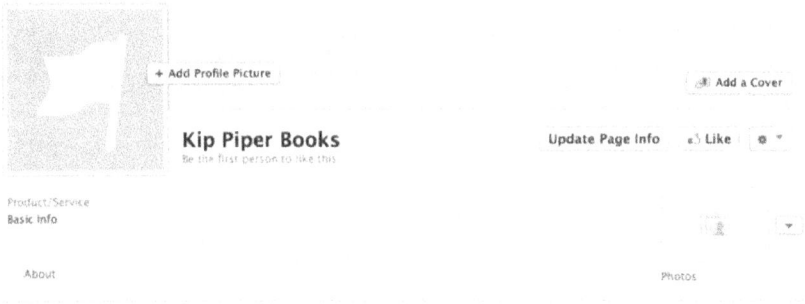

+ Add Profile Picture

Add a Cover

Kip Piper Books

Be the first person to like this

Update Page Info   Like

Product/Service

Basic Info

About   Photos

Now there are a few places I want to show you that you can really optimize and maximize your branding on your page. This is extremely important because it's going to be a reflection of your business.

The first area is your Profile Picture. Now everyone knows how to create a Profile Picture. My point here is that you want to upload an image. You definitely do **not** want to take a picture from your computer and put it up there, and you shouldn't choose from an album.

I recommend you create a custom image for your Profile Picture. Facebook is constantly changing the size requirements for the Profile Picture. You can simply Google the current Facebook Profile Picture size requirement at the time you're reading this book. Your custom image can either be your picture if you are your brand or your business logo.

The second area is your Cover Photo. Again, I recommend that you create a custom image for your Cover Photo.

In your Cover Photo, include the name of your business and a tagline, if you have it. Of course, add your website URL. Now adding your URL to your Cover Photo is *not* a clickable link, but anywhere you can add your website URL, definitely do it!

Finally, you want to add an image to your Cover Photo that is relevant to your business and engages your Facebook visitor and creates curiosity about your business. Again, you can Google for the current Facebook cover photo size requirement at the time you're reading this book.

It is important to remember that Facebook has rules about what you can include in your Cover Photo and your Profile Picture and what you cannot include. Specifically, they have rules about how much of your cover photo Candy text versus how much is in each. If you have to much text, or your text is inappropriate, Facebook can shut down your page. So be sure to Google Facebook's current requirements as far as what your Profile Picture and Cover Photo can contain.

As an example, here is the Facebook page for my affiliate marketing channel:

As you can see, I have a picture of myself as the Profile Picture, and for the Cover Photo I have included the logo from The Random Blonde website as well as the tagline. I have also included a couple of images that reflect what my website is about.

If you're not comfortable designing your own Profile Picture and Cover Photo, there are lots of freelance designers that you could hard to do it for you. You can search on Google for designers, but frankly I and my clients have had great success with using **Fivrr.com http://kippiperbooks.com/Fivrr**. This link is also included in the Resources section at the end of this book.

Remember, your Profile Picture and Cover Photo are the first things that people see when they go to your page, so this is a perfect branding opportunity.

Going back to the creation of my new Facebook page, you will see in the image below in the lower left corner a link to "About". This is the "About" section I referred to earlier.

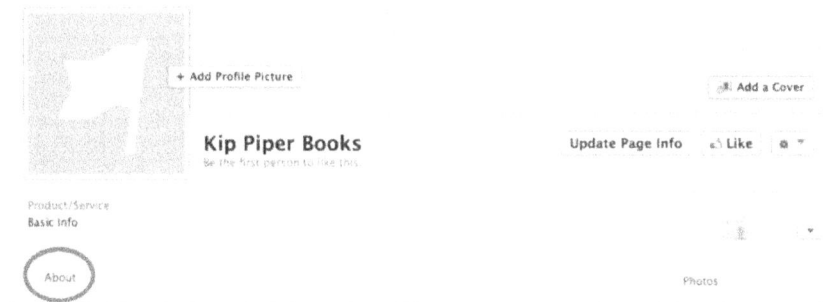

When you click on the "About" link, you come to the screen below.

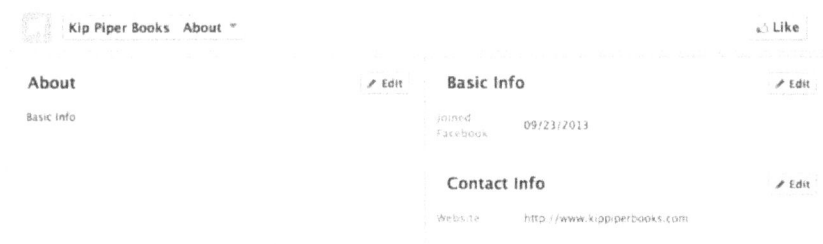

When you hover your mouse over the screen, the "Edit" buttons appear.

When you click on the "Edit" button for "Basic Info", a new screen appears, as you can see below.

Kip Piper Books

‹ View Page

Page Info Settings   Admin Roles   More...

Name	Kip Piper Books	Edit
Page Address	www.facebook.com/kippiperbooks	Edit
Category	Brands & Products Product/Service	Edit
Topics	Choose three words to describe your Page	Edit
Start Info	Joined Facebook	Edit
Release Date	Enter a release date	Edit
Short Description	Basic Info	Edit
Company Overview	Enter company overview	Edit
Long Description	Write a long description for your Page	Edit
General Information	Enter general information	Edit
Mission	Enter mission	Edit
Founded	Enter names of founders	Edit
Awards	Enter awards	Edit
Products	Enter products	Edit
Website	http://www.kippiperbooks.com	Edit
Official Page	Enter the official brand, celebrity or organization your Page is about	Edit

On the "Basic Info" screen, you have the opportunity to answer a wide range of questions about your business. The things that you can edit include when your business was founded, you can write about your business, include a long and short company overviews, plus a wide variety of other items that can add that to your business profile.

Every time that you write about your business, either with the overviews, general description, etc., definitely use keywords in the content for these different sections. Using the keywords would definitely help you be found easier when people do a search for you. These are the best areas to include your keywords.

I encourage you to take advantage of every single space on this "Basic Info" screen. Anywhere where you can put a URL, be sure to include it – of course, as it applies.

All of your areas need to make grammatical sense. So when you're including your keywords and your URL, make sure the content reads well and makes sense.

One item that I want to focus on is your Short Description. When you click on the "Edit" link for Short Description, it will open up with a field for you to complete, as you can see below.

Short Description	Basic Info

Save Changes   Cancel

If you notice, the content includes the words "Basic info", just as I entered them when I was first setting up the Facebook page. Now I can edit and change the content in this field.

What you enter into this field is will appear between your profile picture and the about link on your Facebook page, as you can see below from The Random Blonde Facebook page.

The Random
119 likes · 1 talking abo

Product/Service
The Random Blonde :: Reviews, Articles & Tutorials...
For Your Life, Health, Wealth, Business and Family. Go
to --> www.therandomblonde.com

About

It's really easy to put whatever information you want in this area. But it is critical to remember that the space is very limited. So you want to make sure that whatever you put in the Short Description will fit into the three lines as they appear in the sample above.

The three critical items to include in your short description are: your business/brand name, your tagline, and your URL. (There is no need to add the "http://" in the URL.)

In summary, the "Basic Info" section where I say to spend quality time on. If you have a good copy – not just keywords but good copy – people will go to the "About" tab to learn more about you and your business. This is a great place to showcase who you are and what you're about.

OPTIMIZING YOUR PROFILE:
YOUR BUSINESS PAGE AS YOUR EMPLOYER

In this chapter, we're going to discuss how to get your Facebook page as the main business on your profile. This is extremely important, especially if you're mixing business with pleasure on your Facebook profile. You want to make sure you're showcasing your actual Facebook business page and not a default page that Facebook has set up for your business.

So on my profile under my About section, it list me as an Internet Business Expert at The Random Blonde. When you hover over it, you see a thumbnail of my Facebook page. If you click on the link, you will actually go to my Facebook page.

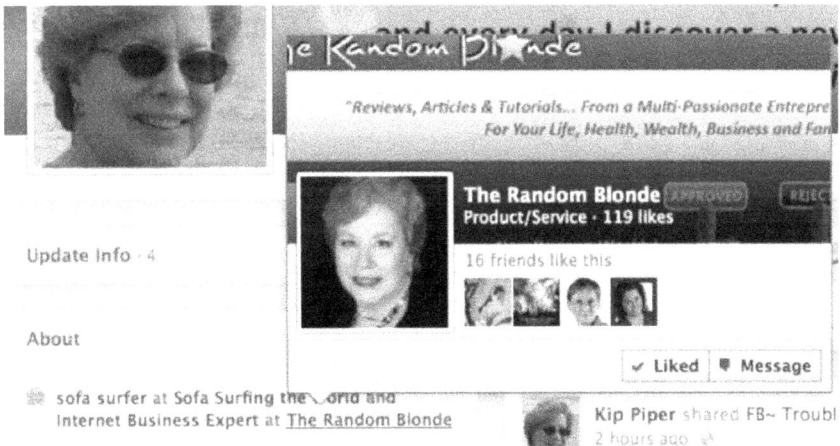

Now to show you something that a lot of people don't realize, here is the work information about one of my friends.

About

💼 Swamper at Light Tower Rentals
Past: Zing Aerosports and Champion Inc.

If you click on the company link of Light Tower Rentals, you will go to a default business page that Facebook automatically generated when my friend said this was where he worked, as you can see below.

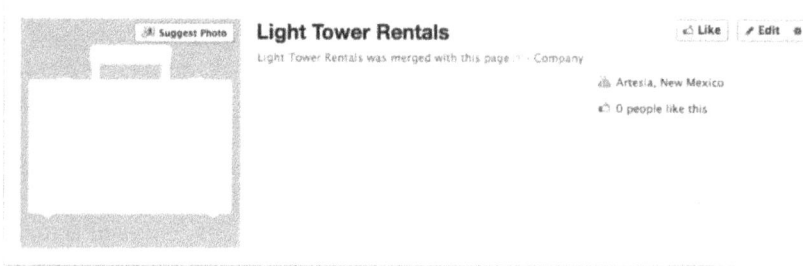

Light Tower Rentals
Light Tower Rentals was merged with this page · Company
👍 Like ✏ Edit
🏢 Artesia, New Mexico
👍 0 people like this
📷 Suggest Photo

Because this is a default page that Facebook is set up, Light Tower Rentals cannot control this page, it's not theirs, and obviously it's not branded at all.

A default Facebook page is the **last** place that you want people to land.

So let me show you how to set up your Facebook page with your profile.

When you edit your profile, under the About section, you will see Work and Education. At the very top is a field that asked the question "Where have you worked?", As you can see below.

Work and Education

Done Editing

Where have you worked?

Sofa Surfing the World
Edit ×
sofa surfer · 2013 to present
As of May 2013, I am "living on the road",
traveling the USA and internationally.

- Add a Project

The Random Blonde
Edit ×
Internet Business Expert · 1993 to present
"Reviews, Articles & Tutorials... From a Multi-
Passionate Entrepreneur ~ For Your Life,
Health, Wealth, Business and Family"

I also work with entrepreneurs and small
business owners to help them build and market
their Internet presence, applying the latest
tools that they can easily use to build their
business.

- Add a Project

In the "Where have you worked?" field, you simply type in the name of your Facebook page. When you see your Facebook page, you click on it and it will automatically be opened within the Work and Education section and is now ready for you to edit and add your relevant information.

It's as simple as that!

Remember, the interface appearance may change, but this function should remain available.

Before I close this chapter, I want to remind you that on your profile make sure you are taking advantage of all the great areas where you can use the keywords for your business. Use these areas to let people know what you do in business, because if your page is mixed with networking people, business acquaintances, in addition to just friends, this information is going to be vital if you want them to be interested in you from a business perspective as well.

So remember, use keywords throughout all of the areas in your profile as much as you can, maximize all of it. Put in as much information as you can, because this will you to get even better reach from your profile.

CUSTOM TABS

In this chapter, we're going to discuss Custom Tabs. Custom Tabs can greatly enhance your Facebook page visitors' experience as well as give you opportunities to engage with your visitors.

A great example of optimizing your Facebook page is with the use of a "Like Us" Custom Tab. Below is a screenshot of Red Bull's custom tab.

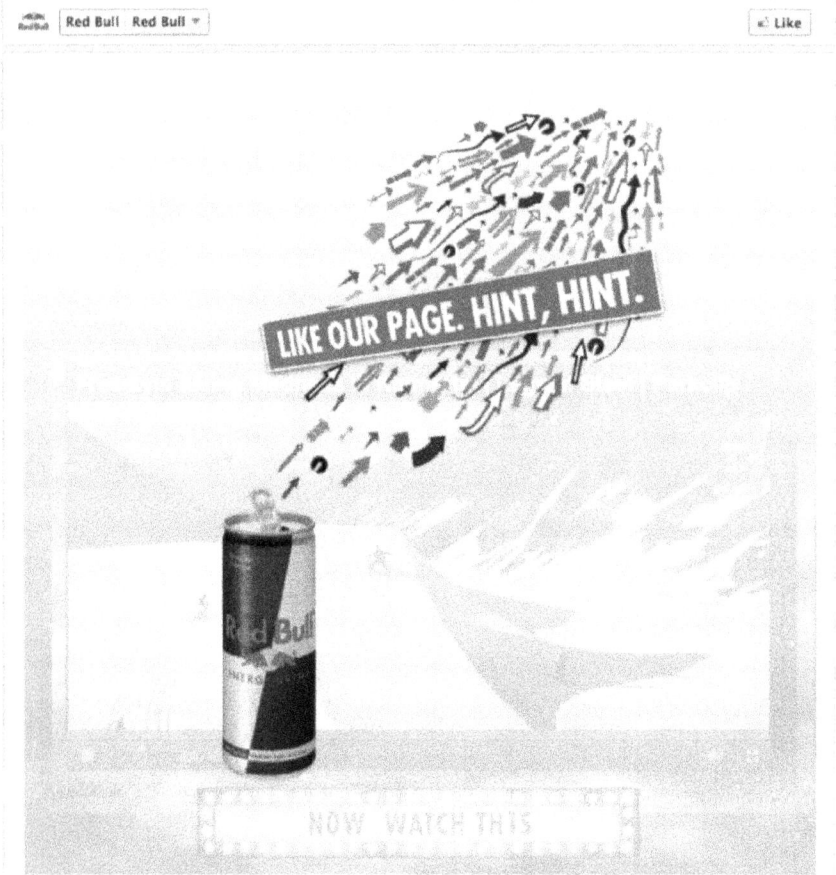

This is about the best custom tab that I have seen in that it has a great call to action. Obviously they want you to click their "Like" button. Once you click their "Like" button, you now have access to exclusive content, as seen below.

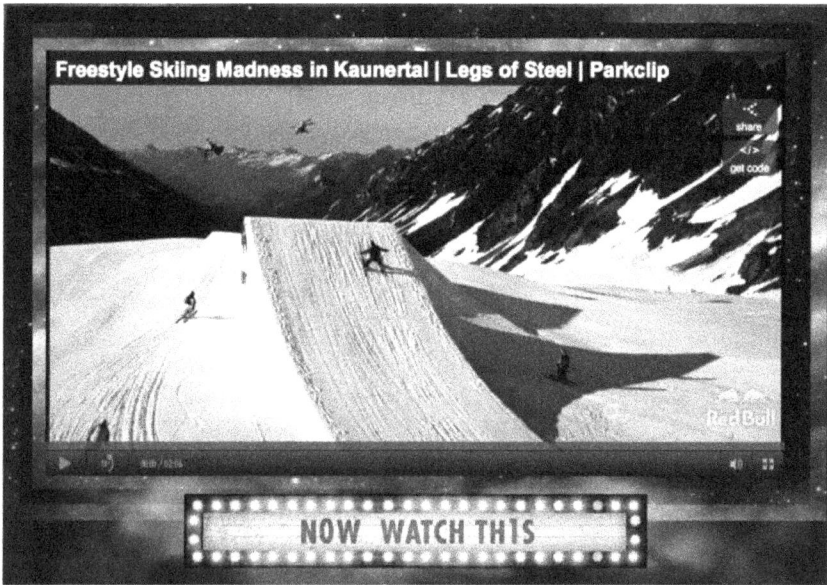

By providing access to exclusive content in this manner, your fans feel special and part of a community – plus, of course, it increases the "Likes" for your Facebook page. It's extremely important to get that "Like".

Another way to use a Custom Tab is to invite your visitors to subscribe to your email list. Below is a shot of Marie Forleo's subscription Custom Tab "Free Life + Business Tips". It is a great example of how to ask for a visitor's name and email while delivering great content in return for that subscription.

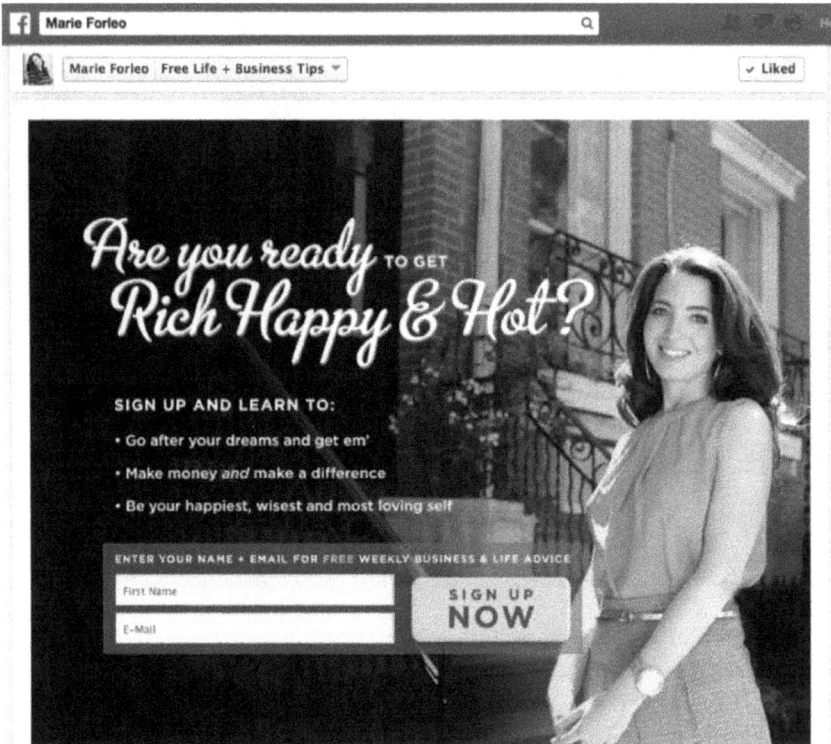

As you know, you should be concentrating on growing your list. Facebook is a great vehicle to do this. As you can see, a Facebook Custom Tab can be extremely customizable and can even include the appropriate code from your email service provider for your visitor to subscribe to your email list.

Here is another great example of the use of a Custom Tab. If you're selling product or you are able to give some kind of discount in a shopping cart, this is also a very smart strategy. What I love about Bealls, as seen below, is that they have an "Exclusive Fan Offer" Custom Tab, which does a great job getting you to click their "Like" button. This is what is called a "Like Gate", "Reveal Tab" or "Fan Only Tab" – in that you have to click on the "Like" button to see what is behind this opening image.

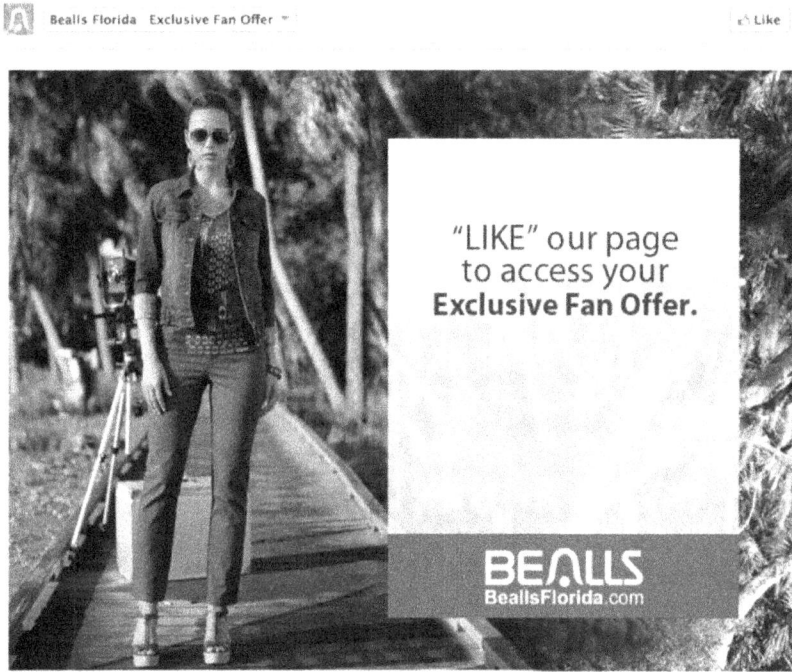

So once you click the "Like" button, you get to see the Exclusive Fan Offer.

As you can see, they then give you a promo code. So you can go to their online shopping cart right away and use that promo code. Really cool!

So if you click on "Shop Now", you will actually be taken out of Facebook and onto their website.

Now I don't always suggest that you take people out of Facebook. I kind of have a rule that, if they're inside Facebook and you want them to click on something, try your hardest to get them to stay within Facebook. So if you can redirect them to another Custom Tab on your Facebook page where there might be a shopping cart, that is a better strategy. Most people don't want to be taken out of Facebook, so you're going to get a lot better results if you keep them where they are already in Facebook.

Another great example about how you can use Custom Tabs is Social Media Examiner. On their Facebook page they have a Custom Tab for "Our Team", as you can see below.

It lists the four people on staff who contribute to their Facebook page on a daily basis. This means that the four people at different times of the day or on the page, answering questions, posting different articles, value add content, and just making it fun for everybody. With that, each staff person signs their name at the end of their post. So if you want to know more about a particular staff person, they have this great Custom Tab for "Our Team".

This is a great strategy if you want to introduce the people who are engaging on your Facebook page from your company. It gives your Facebook visitors a chance to get to know you and your staff a little bit more. The more personal you can make your page, even when you're doing business, the better. This is a great strategy to take personal to the next level and let people read about your team.

The next example I want to show you is, once again, from Amy Porterfield's Facebook page – specifically the Custom Tab for her "Online Class", as you can see below.

This Custom Tab is promoting her **FBInfluence** **http://kippiperbooks.com/FBInfluence** online training course. If Amy were to advertise on Facebook, she can lead people in Facebook to this Custom Tab.

The reason why I love it so much is that it set up in a way that provides really great branding. Right at the top it gives a couple of Amy's credentials and then immediately goes into a headline that gives the benefits of taking the FBInfluence online training course. Then it goes into a really cool video that quickly shows how small business owners and entrepreneurs have harnessed the power of Facebook and use it to increase sales. What is great about this video is that it is relatable – Amy gives real-world examples of people like you and me. This is a dynamically emotional video that is engaging and relevant.

Then if you scroll down, you will see information about the power of Facebook marketing and specific information about Amy's FBInfluence course and the benefits you will realize. Yes, it is a lot of information, but if people are interested in Amy's course, they are going to want to read it. So I feel it's okay that there was a lot of copy because this is an excellent example of a perfectly put together sales letter page.

As you can see, Amy has put her sales letter page from her website right into Facebook on this Custom Tab. As you remember, I mentioned earlier that I believe that you should keep people within Facebook whenever you can. Amy has done this perfectly. You can purchase her course right from this Custom Tab.

This is one of the best Custom Tabs that I've seen to promote an online course. You can use similar techniques if you're promoting an event, whether online or a physical event.

And guess what! Amy not only recommends but also uses the custom tab service **Heyo** **http://kippiperbooks.com/Heyo**. In fact, I use **Heyo** as well and heartily recommend it. **Heyo**'s service offers the easiest way to create campaigns for Facebook that are mobile, tablets, and desktop optimized – with no code required! So even if you are a novice, you can easily build, launch and manage powerful Facebook campaigns. What types of campaigns? Not only does **Heyo** offer standard Custom Tabs, but also Custom Tabs with advanced functionality, such as the "Like Gate" feature to reveal content, Contests, Promotions, and Deals to build your list, and even Ecommerce Stores where you can promote and sell your products and/or affiliate products – all keeping the visitor within the Facebook interface. All of these and more features are available inside the **Heyo** editor interface that is a breeze to use – no code required! Plus new and more powerful features are regularly added! **Heyo** is used by Fortune 500 companies, including NBC, *The Economist*, and Zumba, just to name a few. And **Heyo** offers a 7-day free trial with awesome support to get you started and be successful! I know, a shameless plug. **Heyo** is just that good, and why they are the sponsor of this book!

So these are some examples of how you can use Custom Tabs for your business. It's a great way to get people engaged, to really show your brand, and tell people what you're all about – and also to stand out from other people and businesses that aren't going to make that extra step to make their Facebook page fantastic. When you have these Custom Tabs, it looks like you've gone the extra mile, which is always good for your customers to see.

FACEBOOK SIGNATURE EXPERIENCE

In this chapter we're going to discuss how to create a Facebook Experience, also known as a Signature Experience, for your own Facebook wall.

A Signature Experience is something that you create that is based on your expertise, your knowledge, your content, and the value you add for your fans. It's basically something you create – you make it your own – and you offer immense value to your clients while you're setting yourself up as the expert.

To illustrate what I am talking about, I'm going to give you a few examples that you can pull from, that you can model from, and create your own Signature Experience. The goal is to get your fans engaged, to get more people to see what you're doing, in order to bring them over to your page, to "Like" your page and become your fan, and also just to offer value so you're setting yourself up to your fans as someone that is taking care of them – that you are supporting your fans.

My favorite example of creating a Signature Experience is my friend **Susan K Morrow https://www.facebook.com/psychicsusank**. Susan is a very talented and gifted psychic. Whatever your beliefs, the bottom line is she creates a fabulous signature experience through her monthly live Q&A event called the "Phacebook Phenom".

Susan's Phacebook Phenoms occur at a specific date and time each month. Each Phenom is structured to last just one hour. Susan announces upcoming Phenoms and includes a link for more information, as you can see below. With this post, she is just planting the seed.

Susan K. Morrow
September 7

The Free Facebook Phenom is coming up on Tuesday! Get details here:
http://www.susankmorrow.com/phacebook-phenom-psychic-events/

Like · Comment · Share

What happens the day of, Susan welcomes everyone to the Phenom.

Susan K. Morrow
September 10

It's Phenom time!
PLEASE READ THESE GUIDELINES CAREFULLY FOR A BETTER PHENOM EXPERIENCE!
************ YOU MUST POST YOUR QUESTION AS AN ORIGINAL POST, NOT AS A COMMENT TO THIS POST. PLEASE READ THE REST OF THESE GUIDELINES.*************
* Please, no one under 18. My policy is to have a parent's permission when working with young people.
* Remember that you can make a donation in any amount to h... See More

At that time, Susan is ready to take questions. From that point on, people start posting questions. Each person who joins the Phenom is given the opportunity to ask a question and have it answered – for free! Below is a screenshot of one of her Phenoms. Basically, the participants start firing of questions, and Susan is there to answer them for the next hour.

What is interesting is that people really start getting engaged. As you can see from the screenshot below, Susan answered Rachel's question, Rachel responded, and then Lucero contributed. So there are conversations on the page, not just asking and answering questions. This creates a great community environment.

Rachel Lofsten ▶ **Susan K. Morrow**
June 13 near Sydney, New South Wales, Australia

Hi Susan
Can I please ask for your assistance in cutting all bad ties
with people.
Also will I be successful in completing my degree at uni and
in having children of my own in the future.
Thank you

Like · Comment   👍 1 💬 4

👍 Michael Sherbie likes this.

> **Susan K. Morrow** Hi, Rachel--Cutting all bad ties? Probably
> not entirely possible. You know that the Universe sends you
> what you need and what you attract. And until you get what
> you're supposed to get out of those "bad ties", they ain't goin'
> nowhere! On the other hand, I know several practitioners who
> do "clearing" types of energy work and will be happy to refer
> you, if you like. But I am in favor of getting the message/s
> you're supposed to be getting from these bad ties. Once you
> acknowledge those messages (intended to guide you), they will
> disappear of their own accord. I usually only allow one
> question per person, but I can at least tell you that graduation
> is not too far off! xo Susan
> June 13 at 8:12pm · Like · 👍 1

> **Rachel Lofsten** Thanks Susan I appreciate your incite on
> that.
> June 13 at 8:14pm · Like · 👍 1

> **Lucero Barina** Your intentions and fears create your reality.
> work out your 3rd and 2nd chakras= power and relationship
> with affirmations and taking action
> July 9 at 7:08pm · Like · 👍 2

> **Rachel Lofsten** Thank you Lucero
> July 9 at 7:09pm via mobile · Like

When your community starts engaging and talking among each other, you know you have a thriving community because you're not the one always having to initiate every single conversation. So that's your goal: you want your community talking to each other, not just with you.

Susan's Phacebook Phenoms have proven to be wildly successful, and it's something that you can definitely model. Think about your niche, who's in it, and how you can create a live Q&A event. The cool thing about this is not only does Susan benefit, because she is out there providing a really great service each month and her fans love it, but her fans are getting value from it, plus Susan is getting extra exposure as her fans invite their families and friends to participate. For some of the participants, they really don't know Susan yet, so she gets to introduce herself and bring people over to her website, as well.

Another cool thing is that Susan can gather the Q&As and include them in a blog post later. So you can get extra content as well with this method.

As you can see, there are a lot of great pluses of doing a live Q&A on your Facebook wall. The more real you can make the experiences on your Facebook page, the better they are. That way people can get engaged in the moment, and there's usually more emotion, because people are more excited when talking in real time and going back-and-forth. It's the way we normally communicate anyway, so when you can create those real experiences on your Facebook page, that's when you start getting people engaged and keep coming back for more.

So think about how you can create your own Signature Experiences, create value for your fans, set yourself up as an expert, or just set yourself up as someone who is giving great value back to your fans.

HOW TO CREATE YOUR OWN FACEBOOK SIGNATURE EXPERIENCE

In this chapter, we're going to go over how to create your own Facebook Signature Experiences. I'm going to give you some suggestions, which I hope you will find useful as you start brainstorming ways to create your own Signature Experiences on your Facebook wall.

Decide on the overall vibe you want to create with your Experience

The first step is to decide on the overall vibe you want to create with your Experience. The way you do this is just think:

- Do you want to entertain?
- Do you want to educate?
- Do you want to add value?
- Maybe you want to get your fans excited about something.

Just determine the kind of Experience that will resonate with your fans.

Get clear on what your company does best

The next step is to get clear on what your company does best. The way to do this is you think:

- What do your fans say when they're singing your praises?
- What do they love about you and what you do?

So once you get clear about that – and we all kind of know what is our unique factor – build on that unique factor and really think about what you do best and what you can deliver.

A tip: When you're thinking about the kind of Experience you want to create, think about you can duplicate it on a regular basis. That's the key to these Experiences: it's something that you do more than once, such as something similar to Susan's Phacebook Phenoms every month (or every week), or a Member of the Month, or regularly posting new videos, etc.

So you definitely don't want to do this just once. It's too much work, when done properly, for just a one-time event. You want to make sure you can duplicate it.

Map out your execution plan

Next you want to map out your execution plan. I know this is kind of a pain, and no one really wants to put together a plan, but the way to really increase your fan base – way past 1,000 fans when others only have a few hundred – is to map out everything. I use Google Docs for my clients and myself for everything we do on our respective Facebook pages.

Each Google Doc explains exactly how each Experience is done. If there is to be a guest expert, each guest expert gets a Google Doc that explains how it each Experience is done and how they can prepare for it. So I put together documentation behind each Experience to make it real.

Since you want to execute and duplicate often each Experience, just create a quick document about how you're going to do it and what are the steps to get it done.

Commit to it

The last thing is commit to it. It is so easy to say you're going to do it and not follow through. You started something and you're not following through like you promised your fans. What does that say about your business?

You want to make sure that you follow through when you have your Facebook Experience put together, and you do it as often as you say you're going to do it.

How to optimize your Facebook Experience

Think about how you can repurpose your content. The best thing you can do is take this content and use it other places, such as your blog, in an article, maybe in an audio interview, turn it into an audio file, etc. These are some of the cool things that you can create now that you have extra content to work with.

Hopefully this has generated some ideas on how you can create your own Facebook Experience.

FACEBOOK APPLICATIONS

In this chapter, we're going to go over Facebook Applications.

First, there are thousands and thousands of Facebook Applications. I can guarantee you that about 80% are not Applications that you want for your Facebook business page. It's one thing to have fun on your business page, but it would really random if you were to put a game application, like Farmville or Minecraft, on your page or something like that. You've probably heard of Farmville and Minecraft because they're pretty popular, among others.

But there were some really cool Applications that will work well for your business. The goal is to get you viral visibility. You want to be seen, heard, and interacting everywhere on Facebook – everywhere where it counts. Viral visibility is really important for your brand.

You also want to keep your fans engaged, and Applications do a really good job of getting people to engage and interact on your Facebook page.

Overall, Applications enhance the experience on your Facebook page. With applications, you're making it richer, you're making it better, you're adding value, so it makes your page more interesting.

Where to look for Applications

I don't want to recommend Applications for your business, because Applications come and go and I want you to be able to select the ones that are best for you. In researching Applications for your business, the best place you can go is the **Facebook App Center https://www.facebook.com/appcenter**, as you can see below.

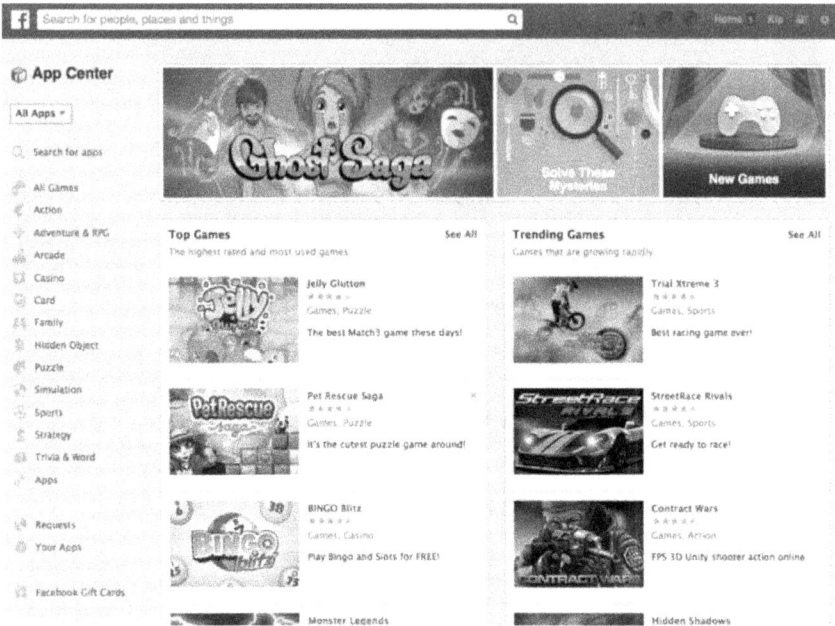

The Facebook App Center will give you every single app you could ever possibly need. It is organized in categories to the left. You can also search for apps with the using the "Search for apps" link at the top left.

There were so many different things that you can do with apps, such as taking polls or running surveys.

North Social http://northsocial.com/apps/ is an excellent website that offers a wide range of very effective and easy to use Facebook Apps.

Also, as you are surfing Facebook and looking at other Facebook pages, look at the Apps that they are using. And search for those Apps and see if they will work with your business.

I also recommend that you search on Google for the best Facebook Apps. PC Magazine and other publications regularly post articles about the best current Facebook Apps.

I realize that telling you to search for your own Apps may seem like a copout, but as I mentioned earlier, Facebook Apps come and go very quickly. So in order for you to be able to take advantage of the best current Facebook Apps available, I recommend that you conduct your own research.

FACEBOOK SOCIAL PLUGINS

In this chapter, we're going to discuss Facebook Social Plugins. Facebook Social Plugins are great because they allow you to take Facebook and put it on your website.

Now remember this: While Facebook is probably not going anywhere, you don't control Facebook. It could shut down tomorrow. You would lose all of your fans. It could also shut down your Facebook page. I have had colleagues who had their Facebook pages shutdown. Facebook's customer service is pretty much nonexistent. So you won't be able to get a hold of Facebook quickly and try to get them to put your Facebook page back up.

You want to be really careful about putting all of your eggs in one basket. You want people from Facebook to eventually move over to your website. So you have fans, you nurture those relationships, you add value, you engage with them, and you build a relationship.

Once you do that, I believe it is safe for you to move them, as much as you can, over to your website. You do that by enticing them with free giveaways, free contact, added value that they have to go to your website to get.

What way to accomplish this is to use Social Plugins. You can have a Facebook experience on your actual website.

Where to you get your social plug-ins? Frankly, the best way is to search for them in the Plugins area of your blog-format website. The search function is not completely intuitive, but with a little persistence, you will be able to find a selection of Plugins for just about any function. Be sure to choose Plugins that have at least a 4- star rating. This way you can be sure that it is a stable Plugin that should work well with your site.

What plug-ins should you use, here I will discuss a few that I think are very important as Facebook Social Plugins.

One thing I think everyone should have on their website is a Facebook "Like" box. As you can see below, Amy Porterfield's homepage has a Facebook "Like" box on the right side.

Join Me On Facebook!

#017: 7 Facebook Changes That Affect Your Business Today

September 12, 2013 By Amy • 9 Comments

Amy Porterfield

Like

47.119 people like Amy Porterfield.

156   91   11   s   37

Like   Tweet   +1   Pin it   Buffer

Online Marketing Made Easy

Facebook gives me plenty of opportunity to create content because they are notorious for making updates to their platform! There have been a lot of pretty significant Facebook changes in the past few months, so on this episode of the Online Marketing

Facebook social plugin

As you can see, there is a live "Like" button in this plug-in. When a visitor clicks the "Like", they automatically like your Facebook page without having to redirect them to Facebook page in order to do so.

What is very cool about a Facebook "Like" box Plugin is that you can adjust the size and the amount of information that is shown on your website. You can incorporate your fans pictures, and you can incorporate your comments and posts from your Facebook page. The important thing is that your website visitors can like your Facebook page without leaving your website.

This is a great way to grow your fans and showcase your Facebook page from your own website.

Where else can you find Facebook Social Plugins? It's very simple. As you surf the Internet and check out other websites within your niche, take a look at what Social Plugins they are using on their websites. If you feel a Social Plugin would be valuable for you, your website visitors, and your Facebook fans, then research it and try it out on your website. And yes, you can have multiple Facebook Social Plugins on your website. Just be sure you're not duplicating the experience but rather enriching it with multiple Social Plugins.

As you can see there are several ways you can enhance the Facebook experience. You can use a variety of applications and social plug-ins, with the goal of getting people more engaged and interactive with you and your fans. The more you do that, the more your fans will like and trust you and Bill want to do business with you.

SUMMARY

Now that we have gone through the different ways you can build your list with Facebook, here is what's important about Facebook.

Obviously you need to set up a regular Facebook profile page, if you haven't already.

You need have a Facebook business page or fan page in place.

You also need to look at, explore and find Facebook groups within your niche. You can use the Facebook search feature to find groups in your niche.

The average Facebook user is on Facebook at least once every single day, and spends an average of 30 minutes every single day on Facebook. That is a massive amount of potential traffic.

Facebook is a great way to build a connection with our lists – both friends and fans.

As I mentioned in the Introduction, the most important part of including Facebook in your marketing strategy is not just communicating with people on Facebook. As information and Internet marketers, we need a better place to market to our list.

Facebook is *not* the best place to market. However, it is a great place to build a connection with your audience and help us build a general Internet presence.

Why? It's free. There's over 1 billion users on Facebook.

What you need to focus on is taking your friends, your Likes, and the people you connect with in groups, and bringing them over to your email list so you can market to them in a more targeted fashion. Then you can sell them either your product. or affiliate products and offers.

Remember, sending people from Facebook – whether it's from your profile page or your Facebook business page – directly to your offer is *not* the best strategy.

So you need to make sure you have a clearly defined strategy and how you can get those people from your Facebook profile and Facebook business page to your email list.

As mentioned in the Introduction, any time you write a blog post, you're going to want to share a link to that blog on your Facebook profile, Facebook page, and even in your groups.

As an important part of the process when you send people to a blog post, you need to make sure that you have your opt-in offer clearly visible. So not only are you giving them free information in the content of that blog post, it's important that you have an opportunity to capture their name and email.

Another way to capture their name and email is to send them to the promotion of an event you may be doing, such as a webinar, a Q&A event, etc.

Webinars are a great way to sell products and services, and promote affiliate offers. But webinars are probably one of the best ways take a free presence like Facebook and convert that free presence to your email list.

What happens when someone registers for a webinar? They have to complete an online form with their name and email. So it's a great way to convert that traffic from your Facebook profile and Facebook business page specifically into your email list.

This is what it's all about. We talked about in this book how to set up your Facebook profile and Facebook business page, how to interact with your friends and fans, and add enhancements to the experience. Ultimately you want to take that information and be strategic in what you're doing and convert that traffic and that presence into an email list.

Remember, the reason sending people directly to a sales page for a product or an affiliate offer is not a good strategy is because people are not used to seeing offers directly on Facebook. If you do this, the traffic will not convert as well.

To sum it up, get your Facebook friends and fans from your Facebook presence – whether it's from your profile page, fan page or your groups – onto your email list using the strategies we discussed in this book.

BONUS MATERIALS

Below is the link to this book's bonus material. I have developed this tools from my own experience as well as compiled from tools I have used from various training courses I have taken.

The mind map is built in XMind software. You can download a free version of XMind from http://www.xmind.net.

The item is also available as a PDF.

Strategic_Plan_List_Building_with_Facebook.xmind
http://www.kippiperbooks.com/make-money-online/book08/Strategic_Plan_List_Building_with_Facebook.xmind

Strategic_Plan_List_Building_with_Facebook.pdf
http://www.kippiperbooks.com/make-money-online/book08/Strategic_Plan_List_Building_with_Facebook.pdf

RESOURCES

FBInfluence by Amy Porterfield

http://kippiperbooks.com/FBInfluence

This course teaches you how to create a Facebook page for your business and optimize it for the most marketing value.

Heyo *(Official Sponsor)*

http://kippiperbooks.com/heyo

Heyo is the most valuable social-marketing platform available for conversion-focused businesses. We make creating social media campaigns fast and easy with pre-built templates and a simple, drag-and-drop campaign builder. The Heyo platform is also backed by fanatical customer support to ensure you are always in good hands.

Fivrr

http://kippiperbooks.com/Fivrr

Great inexpensive source for logos, graphics, writers, marketers, etc.

North Social

http://northsocial.com/apps/

Great website for many effective and easy to use Facebook Apps.

MORE KINDLE BOOKS BY KIP PIPER

Ultimate Affiliate Marketing with Blogging Quick Start Guide
http://www.kippiperbooks.com/UltimateGuide

Make Money Online Entrepreneur Series:

Below are just a few of the books in this series. To browse the entire series, go to: **http://www.kippiperbooks.com/makemoneyonlineseries**

Book 1 – Freeing Up Your Time – VA's, Outsourcing & Goal Setting
http://www.kippiperbooks.com/book1

Book 2 – Your Core Business, Niche & Competitors
http://www.kippiperbooks.com/book2

Book 3 – Blogs & Emails: Your Link with Your Customers
http://www.kippiperbooks.com/book3

Book 4 – Affiliate Marketing 101
http://www.kippiperbooks.com/book4

Book 5 - Driving Traffic with Organic SEO
http://www.kippiperbooks.com/book5

Book 6 – Power of Email Marketing
http://www.kippiperbooks.com/book6

Book 7 – Quick Income Formula with Advanced Affiliate Marketing
http://www.kippiperbooks.com/book7

Book 8 – List Building with Facebook
http://www.kippiperbooks.com/book8

Book 9 – List Building with Twitter
http://www.kippiperbooks.com/book9

Book 10 - List Building with LinkedIn
http://www.kippiperbooks.com/book10

ONE LAST THING…

As you can probably tell from my writing, my intention is to inspire and support more people to build a better financial future. It's a tough economy today, and I think personal growth in the field of small business is more important than ever before. Even though I have well over 20 years of experience as a successful small business owner and online entrepreneur, I don't have all the answers. In fact I'm still learning myself, I just have my own opinions, experiences and a passion for being my own boss to guide me through life.

Thank you purchasing my eBook and for taking the time to read it. I hope you enjoyed it and found value within its pages.

If you did I would really appreciate your support by taking the time to write a review for me on Amazon. Reviews really help the authors you enjoy to get noticed in a crowded marketplace, and it would allow me to continue writing the books for this series and other business books.

Please visit the URL below to let me know your thoughts:

http://kippiperbooks.com/book8

All of my books are offered completely FREE on the launch and I want to reward loyal readers by offering my new books to them FREE of charge when they are released.

So please visit my website KipPiperBooks.com and either download your free copy of "28-Day Small Business Profit Plan: The Quick Start Guide to Business Success" or just sign up to my newsletter in order to be kept informed when the next release is due. I hate spam, so I promise I won't share your information with anyone – not for love nor money!

Good luck! I wish you every success in your personal and business endeavors.

www.ingramcontent.com/pod-product-compliance
Lightning Source LLC
Chambersburg PA
CBHW070811210326
41520CB00011B/1906